K. CONNORS

Influencer Marketing Guide

Strategies, Tips, and Best Practices for Growing Your Brand, Increasing Sales, and Boosting Online Visibility

First edition

This book was professionally typeset on Reedsy.
Find out more at reedsy.com

Contents

Introduction 1
Chapter 1: Finding the Right Influencers for Your Brand 7
Chapter 2: Building Relationships with Influencers 12
Chapter 3: Creating Effective Influencer Campaigns 16
Chapter 4: Legal Considerations and Contracts 21
Chapter 5: Measuring the ROI of Influencer Marketing 26
Chapter 6: Micro-Influencers vs. Macro-Influencers 31
Chapter 7: Influencer Marketing on Different Platforms 36
Chapter 8: Case Studies of Successful Influencer Campaigns 42
Chapter 9: The Future of Influencer Marketing 48
Chapter 10: Navigating Challenges in Influencer Marketing 54
Conclusion 59

Introduction

Influencer marketing is no longer a buzzword; it's a powerful strategy reshaping the landscape of digital marketing. In a world where traditional advertising often feels intrusive or easily ignored, influencers have become the trusted voices that consumers listen to. They are the new-age brand ambassadors, connecting with audiences in a way that feels authentic, relatable, and, most importantly, influential. But how did we get here? What is it about influencers that makes them so effective, and how can brands harness this power to their advantage?

The roots of influencer marketing stretch back further than Instagram or YouTube. Before social media, there were celebrities endorsing products on television, in magazines, and on billboards. Brands would pay top dollar for a recognizable face to hawk their wares, relying on the star's fame to drive sales. It was a straightforward equation: celebrity + product = consumer trust. However, as audiences became savvier and more skeptical, this formula started to lose its effectiveness. Enter the influencer.

Influencers are, at their core, individuals who have built a following through content creation, often in specific niches. They aren't famous in the traditional sense; instead, they are known for their expertise, authenticity, and ability to connect with their audience on a personal level. Whether it's a beauty guru demonstrating the latest makeup techniques, a fitness enthusiast sharing workout routines, or a tech reviewer unboxing the latest gadgets, influencers have cultivated communities around their passions. These communities are engaged, loyal, and, crucially, trust the influencer's opinions and recommendations.

What makes influencer marketing particularly compelling is this trust. When an influencer endorses a product, it doesn't feel like an ad; it feels like a recommendation from a friend. This trust translates into significant power. Studies have shown that consumers are more likely to purchase a product recommended by an influencer than through traditional advertising channels. This shift in consumer behavior has led brands to pivot their marketing strategies, investing more in influencer partnerships to reach their target audiences in a meaningful way.

Identifying the right influencers is the first step in a successful influencer marketing strategy. It's not just about finding someone with a large following; it's about finding someone whose audience aligns with your brand's target market. A beauty brand, for example, would benefit more from partnering with a makeup artist who has a smaller but highly engaged following than with a celebrity who rarely posts about beauty. The key is relevance and engagement, not just reach.

When evaluating potential influencers, it's essential to look beyond the numbers. Sure, follower count is an important metric, but it's not the only one. Engagement rate—how often followers like, comment, or share an influencer's content—is a far more telling indicator of an influencer's impact. A large following with low engagement might suggest that the influencer's audience isn't as invested, which could lead to lackluster campaign results. On the other hand, an influencer with a smaller, highly engaged audience might drive better results because their followers are more likely to act on their recommendations.

Another critical factor to consider is the influencer's content style and values. Their tone, aesthetics, and messaging should align with your brand's identity. A mismatch here could result in a campaign that feels disjointed or inauthentic, which could damage both the influencer's credibility and your brand's reputation. It's crucial to spend time researching and vetting potential influencers, reviewing their content, and understanding how they interact with their audience before reaching out.

Once you've identified the right influencers, the next step is building a relationship with them. Influencer marketing is not a one-off transaction; it's a partnership that should be nurtured over time. The best influencer-brand collaborations are those where both parties feel valued and respected. This begins with clear and open communication. Brands should be transparent about their goals, expectations, and the kind of support they can provide. In turn, influencers should feel comfortable sharing their ideas and feedback.

Negotiating partnerships with influencers can be a delicate process. Compensation is, of course, a significant factor, but it's not the only one. Influencers often value creative control, and for good reason—their followers trust them because of their authentic voice. Too much brand interference can make content feel forced or unnatural, which can turn off audiences. Striking a balance where the influencer feels they have the freedom to create while still aligning with the brand's objectives is key to a successful partnership.

Compensation can take many forms, from flat fees and product exchanges to performance-based incentives. Some influencers might prefer upfront payment, while others might be open to commission-based arrangements where they earn a percentage of the sales generated from their content. It's important to discuss these options openly and find a mutually beneficial arrangement. Additionally, consider offering influencers perks like exclusive previews of new products, VIP access to events, or opportunities to co-create products. These can strengthen the partnership and make the influencer feel more invested in your brand's success.

Legal considerations also play a crucial role in influencer marketing. Contracts should outline the terms of the partnership, including deliverables, timelines, compensation, and disclosure requirements. It's important to ensure that influencers disclose their partnership with your brand in a way that complies with legal guidelines, such as the Federal Trade Commission (FTC) rules in the United States. Failure to do so can lead to penalties for both the brand and the influencer and can erode consumer trust. A well-drafted contract protects both parties and sets clear expectations, reducing the likelihood of misunderstandings or disputes.

Measuring the success of influencer marketing campaigns is another area where brands need to focus. Unlike traditional advertising, where metrics like impressions and click-through rates are straightforward, influencer marketing success can be more nuanced. It's not just about how many people saw the influencer's post; it's about how many engaged with it, how many visited your website, and ultimately, how many made a purchase. Tracking these metrics requires a combination of tools and techniques, from UTM codes and affiliate links to social media analytics and surveys.

ROI in influencer marketing isn't always immediate, especially for campaigns focused on brand awareness rather than direct sales. However, by tracking the right metrics, brands can gain valuable insights into how their campaigns are performing and where adjustments might be needed. It's also important to consider qualitative feedback, such as the sentiment of comments on influencer posts and the types of questions or concerns raised by the audience. This feedback can offer deeper insights into how your brand is perceived and how you can improve future campaigns.

One of the most debated topics in influencer marketing is the choice between working with micro-influencers and macro-influencers. Micro-influencers typically have smaller, more niche audiences, but they often boast higher engagement rates and a more personal connection with their followers. Macro-influencers, on the other hand, have broader reach but may come with a hefty price tag and a less engaged audience. The decision largely depends on your campaign goals and budget. If you're looking to drive conversions or tap into a specific community, micro-influencers might be the way to go. For broad brand awareness, a macro-influencer might be more effective.

Different social media platforms also play a significant role in influencer marketing. Instagram has long been the go-to platform for influencers, thanks to its visual nature and high engagement rates. However, other platforms like YouTube, TikTok, and even LinkedIn are becoming increasingly important. Each platform has its strengths: YouTube is great for long-form content and detailed reviews, TikTok is ideal for reaching younger audiences with short, viral videos, and LinkedIn is the place to be for B2B influencers and industry thought leaders. Understanding the nuances of each platform can help you choose the right influencers and craft campaigns that resonate with the audience on that platform.

Case studies of successful influencer campaigns can offer valuable lessons and inspiration. For example, when Glossier launched their beauty brand, they focused on micro-influencers and regular customers to build a community around their products, which led to rapid growth and a loyal customer base. On the other hand, Nike's collaboration with Colin Kaepernick, a macro-influencer in his own right, generated massive brand awareness and sparked important conversations around social justice. These examples show that there is no one-size-fits-all approach to influencer marketing; success comes from understanding your brand, your audience, and how to connect the two through the right influencers.

Looking to the future, influencer marketing shows no signs of slowing down. As social media platforms evolve and new ones emerge, influencers will continue to play a pivotal role in shaping consumer behavior. However, the industry is likely to see changes, such as increased regulation, the rise of AI-powered virtual influencers, and a greater focus on long-term partnerships rather than one-off collaborations. Brands that stay ahead of these trends and continue to adapt their strategies will be well-positioned to succeed in the ever-changing world of influencer marketing.

Chapter 1: Finding the Right Influencers for Your Brand

Finding the right influencers for your brand is more than just scrolling through Instagram or TikTok and picking someone with a large following. It's about identifying individuals who align with your brand's values, resonate with your target audience, and have the ability to convey your message authentically. In today's digital landscape, where consumers are increasingly skeptical of traditional advertising, the choice of influencer can make or break a campaign. This chapter explores the nuances of selecting the right influencers, offering insights into the factors that should guide your decision-making process.

First and foremost, it's crucial to understand that not all influencers are created equal. While follower count is often the first metric that brands look at, it's far from the most important. An influencer with a million followers might seem like an obvious choice, but if those followers are not engaged or don't fit your target demographic, your efforts (and budget) could be wasted. Engagement rate is a far more telling metric—how often do followers like, comment, share, or otherwise interact with the influencer's content? A smaller, highly engaged audience is often more valuable than a large, passive one.

When evaluating potential influencers, relevance is key. An influencer who is deeply embedded in your industry or niche is likely to have a more authentic connection with their audience, and by extension, your brand. For instance, a fitness brand would do well to partner with a personal trainer who regularly shares workout tips and healthy lifestyle content, rather than a general lifestyle influencer who occasionally posts about fitness. The more relevant the influencer's content is to your brand, the more likely their followers will be interested in what you have to offer.

Another critical aspect to consider is the influencer's content style and voice. Every influencer has a unique way of communicating with their audience, whether it's through humor, storytelling, or a highly polished aesthetic. Their tone should complement your brand's personality. If your brand is fun and playful, an influencer known for their witty, light-hearted content might be a perfect fit. Conversely, if your brand is more serious and professional, an influencer with a more polished and informative approach might be more appropriate. The goal is to ensure that the partnership feels natural and that the influencer can seamlessly integrate your brand into their content.

In addition to content style, the values and ethics of the influencer are increasingly important. Today's consumers are more socially conscious and are likely to scrutinize the brands and individuals they follow. An influencer who shares your brand's values—whether that's a commitment to sustainability, social justice, or innovation—can help you connect with like-minded audiences. On the flip side, partnering with an influencer whose values clash with your brand's can lead to backlash and damage your reputation. It's essential to do your due diligence, researching not just the influencer's content but also their broader online presence and past collaborations.

The next step is assessing the influencer's audience demographics. Knowing who their followers are will help you determine whether the influencer can effectively reach your target market. Factors to consider include the age, gender, location, and interests of their audience. Many influencers provide media kits that include detailed audience analytics, which can be incredibly useful. However, it's also worth taking a closer look at their followers' comments and interactions to get a sense of who they are and how they engage with the content.

Another aspect of finding the right influencers is understanding the different types of influencers and what they bring to the table. Broadly speaking, influencers can be categorized into four groups: mega-influencers, macro-influencers, micro-influencers, and nano-influencers. Each category has its own strengths and challenges.

Mega-influencers are typically celebrities or individuals with millions of followers. They offer extensive reach and can generate significant brand awareness. However, they often come with a high price tag, and their large audiences can be quite diverse, meaning their content might not resonate with all of their followers. Additionally, the engagement rates of mega-influencers can be lower compared to those with smaller followings.

Macro-influencers have followings that range from hundreds of thousands to a million. They still offer considerable reach but are often more affordable than mega-influencers. They tend to have more focused content niches, which can make them a good choice for brands looking to target specific audiences.

Micro-influencers typically have between 10,000 to 100,000 followers. What they lack in reach, they make up for in engagement and authenticity. Micro-influencers often have strong connections with their followers, who see them as trusted sources of information rather than celebrities. For many brands, especially those with niche products or services, micro-influencers can offer the best return on investment.

Nano-influencers are the smallest category, with fewer than 10,000 followers. Despite their limited reach, they often have highly engaged and loyal audiences. Nano-influencers are particularly effective for hyper-local or very niche markets. They're also more accessible and willing to work with smaller budgets, making them a great option for small businesses or brands looking to build grassroots support.

Once you've identified a shortlist of potential influencers, the next step is to engage with them. Building a relationship with an influencer is not just about pitching a business proposition; it's about creating a partnership based on mutual respect and shared goals. Start by following them on social media, engaging with their content, and getting to know their style and preferences. This will not only help you better understand their audience but also show the influencer that you're genuinely interested in what they do.

When you're ready to reach out, make sure your pitch is personalized. Influencers receive countless collaboration requests, so a generic message is likely to be ignored. Highlight why you think they're a great fit for your brand, what you admire about their content, and how you envision working together. Be clear about what you can offer in return, whether it's monetary compensation, free products, or something more creative like exclusive event invitations or a long-term ambassadorship.

Negotiating the terms of the partnership is a crucial step. Compensation can vary widely depending on the influencer's reach, engagement, and the scope of the campaign. Some influencers may charge a flat fee per post, while others might prefer a commission-based arrangement, where they earn a percentage of the sales generated through their content. It's also worth considering other forms of compensation, such as product exchanges, which can be particularly appealing to influencers who are genuinely interested in your brand.

In addition to compensation, it's important to discuss the creative direction of the campaign. While you may have specific goals and messaging in mind, giving the influencer creative freedom is often the key to a successful partnership. After all, they know their audience better than anyone and will have a sense of what will resonate. Too much brand interference can make the content feel forced or inauthentic, which can turn off their followers. The best influencer collaborations are those where both parties feel they have a say in the content creation process.

Once the campaign is underway, it's essential to maintain open lines of communication. Regular check-ins can help ensure that everything is on track and that both parties are satisfied with the progress. It's also a good idea to monitor the influencer's content closely, not just to ensure they're meeting their deliverables, but to gauge the audience's response. Are followers engaging with the content? Are they asking questions or showing interest in your brand? This kind of real-time feedback can be invaluable in adjusting your strategy as needed.

Finally, after the campaign concludes, take the time to review its performance. Look beyond vanity metrics like likes and shares, and focus on the tangible results—how many leads or sales were generated, how much traffic was driven to your website, and whether the campaign had any long-term impact on brand awareness or loyalty. This data will not only help you assess the success of the current campaign but also inform future influencer partnerships.

Finding the right influencers for your brand is a process that requires careful consideration, research, and strategy. It's not just about finding someone with a large following; it's about finding someone who truly embodies your brand's values, speaks to your target audience, and can create content that feels genuine and engaging. By taking the time to choose the right influencers, you can create powerful partnerships that drive real results for your brand.

Chapter 2: Building Relationships with Influencers

Building relationships with influencers goes beyond a simple transactional exchange. It's about creating a partnership that feels authentic and mutually beneficial, where both the brand and the influencer are invested in each other's success. In the fast-paced world of social media, where trends change in the blink of an eye and audiences crave authenticity, the strength of your relationship with influencers can be the key to unlocking the full potential of influencer marketing.

At the heart of any strong relationship is trust. This is especially true in influencer marketing, where trust between the influencer and their audience is the foundation upon which their influence is built. For a brand to tap into that influence effectively, the relationship must be grounded in genuine trust and respect. This means approaching influencers not just as another marketing tool, but as creative partners whose voice, style, and vision are integral to the success of the campaign.

The first step in building a strong relationship with influencers is to start with genuine engagement. Before you even think about sending that first collaboration email, take the time to engage with their content. Follow them on their social media platforms, like and comment on their posts, and show an interest in their work. This isn't about flattery; it's about understanding who they are as content creators and what resonates with their audience. By actively engaging with their content, you demonstrate that you value their work and are genuinely interested in what they do, which can make them more receptive to a potential partnership.

Once you've established a presence in their world, the next step is to approach them with a personalized and thoughtful pitch. A generic, one-size-fits-all message is unlikely to capture the attention of an influencer who probably receives dozens of collaboration requests. Instead, craft a message that reflects your understanding of their work and explains why you believe they are the perfect fit for your brand. Highlight specific aspects of their content that align with your brand values, and outline how you envision working together. This level of personalization shows that you've done your homework and are serious about creating a meaningful partnership.

When approaching influencers, transparency is crucial. Be clear about your expectations, including the goals of the campaign, the deliverables, and any timelines you have in mind. However, it's equally important to allow room for the influencer's creativity and input. After all, they know their audience best and can offer valuable insights into what will resonate. By involving them in the planning process, you not only show respect for their expertise but also increase the likelihood of a successful campaign.

Compensation is another critical element in building a strong relationship with influencers. It's important to approach this aspect with fairness and flexibility. While some influencers might have set rates, others might be open to negotiation based on the scope of the work or the potential for a long-term partnership. Beyond monetary compensation, consider offering additional perks such as early access to new products, invitations to exclusive events, or opportunities for cross-promotion. These gestures can go a long way in making the influencer feel valued and appreciated, which can foster a more collaborative and enthusiastic relationship.

As the relationship progresses, maintaining open and ongoing communication is key. Regular check-ins can help ensure that both parties are aligned and that the campaign is on track. These check-ins don't have to be formal; sometimes, a quick message or a brief call can be enough to address any questions or concerns. This ongoing dialogue also provides an opportunity to discuss any adjustments that might be needed as the campaign evolves, ensuring that the content remains relevant and engaging for the audience.

One of the most important aspects of building relationships with influencers is the recognition that these partnerships should be seen as long-term investments rather than one-off transactions. Developing a sustained relationship with an influencer allows both the brand and the influencer to grow together, creating a deeper connection with the audience over time. Long-term collaborations can also lead to more authentic content, as the influencer becomes more familiar with your brand and can integrate it more seamlessly into their storytelling.

To further strengthen the relationship, brands can involve influencers in more significant aspects of their marketing strategy. For example, some brands have successfully co-created products with influencers, allowing them to design a limited-edition line or curate a collection. This not only deepens the influencer's connection to the brand but also creates a unique selling point that can attract both the influencer's audience and new customers. Such collaborations are a testament to the power of a well-nurtured influencer relationship, where both parties are fully invested in the success of the partnership.

However, as with any relationship, challenges can arise. It's important to be prepared for potential issues and handle them with professionalism and empathy. If an influencer misses a deadline or doesn't deliver the expected quality of content, approach the situation with understanding and a focus on finding a solution. Similarly, if an influencer expresses concerns about the campaign, take their feedback seriously and be willing to make adjustments if necessary. By addressing challenges collaboratively, you can strengthen the relationship and build a foundation of mutual respect and trust.

In the end, the success of your influencer marketing efforts hinges not just on the influencers you choose, but on the relationships you build with them. A strong, positive relationship can lead to more impactful campaigns, greater brand loyalty, and a more authentic connection with your audience. It's about seeing influencers not just as a means to an end, but as true partners who can help you achieve your marketing goals while also elevating their own brand. By investing time and effort into nurturing these relationships, you can unlock the full potential of influencer marketing and create campaigns that resonate deeply with consumers.

In summary, building relationships with influencers is an essential part of any successful influencer marketing strategy. It requires a commitment to engagement, transparency, and mutual respect. By approaching influencers as creative partners and involving them in the planning process, you can create more authentic and effective campaigns. Compensation should be fair and flexible, with an emphasis on long-term collaboration rather than one-off transactions. Regular communication and a willingness to address challenges collaboratively are also key to maintaining strong relationships. When done right, these relationships can lead to powerful partnerships that drive significant results for both the brand and the influencer.

Chapter 3: Creating Effective Influencer Campaigns

Creating effective influencer campaigns requires more than just finding the right influencers and building relationships with them. It's about crafting a strategy that seamlessly integrates the influencer's voice with your brand's message, ensuring that the content resonates with the target audience and achieves the desired outcomes. In an era where consumers are inundated with content, the challenge lies in standing out while maintaining authenticity. This chapter delves into the nuances of developing successful influencer campaigns, offering insights into the planning, execution, and optimization processes that drive results.

The foundation of any successful influencer campaign begins with a clear understanding of your goals. Before you even start thinking about the creative aspects of the campaign, it's essential to define what you want to achieve. Are you looking to increase brand awareness, drive traffic to your website, boost sales, or perhaps all three? Each of these goals requires a different approach, and understanding them will guide every subsequent decision in the campaign development process.

Once your goals are clearly defined, the next step is to identify the target audience. This might seem obvious, but it's a critical step that can often be overlooked in the excitement of partnering with an influencer. The influencer's audience should align closely with your target market, not just in terms of demographics but also in terms of interests, values, and behaviors. Understanding who you're trying to reach will help you and the influencer create content that resonates on a deeper level.

With your goals and target audience in mind, you can begin to develop the campaign's core message. This message should be simple, clear, and aligned with both your brand's values and the influencer's personal brand. It's important to strike a balance between promoting your product or service and allowing the influencer to maintain their authentic voice. The best campaigns are those where the promotional content feels natural and integrated, rather than forced or overly salesy.

Creative direction is another critical aspect of campaign development. While it's important to provide influencers with clear guidelines and expectations, it's equally important to allow them creative freedom. Influencers are content creators, and they understand what works best for their audience. By trusting them to interpret your brand message in a way that feels authentic to their style, you're more likely to see content that resonates and engages. This might mean letting go of some control, but the trade-off is content that feels more genuine and less like an ad.

A key element of creative direction is deciding on the type of content that will be most effective for your campaign. Different types of content serve different purposes, and the choice should be guided by your campaign goals. For instance, a series of Instagram Stories might be perfect for a time-sensitive promotion, while a long-form YouTube video might be better suited for an in-depth product review. Similarly, a TikTok challenge could be ideal for generating buzz and user-generated content, while a blog post might be more appropriate for conveying detailed information about a product or service. The choice of content format should also take into account the strengths of the influencer and the platform they're most active on.

Another important consideration is the timing of the campaign. Launching a campaign at the right time can significantly impact its success. Factors to consider include seasonal trends, industry events, and the influencer's own content calendar. For example, a fitness brand might want to align a campaign with the start of the new year, when health and wellness resolutions are top of mind for many people. Similarly, a fashion brand might plan a campaign around key shopping periods like Black Friday or the start of the summer season. Timing can also affect the logistics of the campaign, such as product availability and shipping times, so it's important to plan accordingly.

The next phase of creating an effective influencer campaign is execution. This is where all the planning comes to life, and attention to detail is crucial. Clear communication is key during this stage, both with the influencer and within your own team. Ensure that everyone is on the same page regarding timelines, deliverables, and any potential challenges that might arise. It's also a good idea to have a contingency plan in place in case something doesn't go as expected.

During the execution phase, it's important to monitor the campaign closely. This doesn't mean micromanaging the influencer's every move, but rather staying engaged and responsive. Be available to answer questions, provide additional resources, or make adjustments if necessary. Monitoring also involves keeping an eye on the campaign's performance as it unfolds. Tracking engagement metrics, such as likes, comments, shares, and views, can provide valuable insights into how the audience is responding to the content. This real-time feedback can be used to make adjustments on the fly, optimizing the campaign for better results.

Another critical aspect of execution is ensuring compliance with legal and ethical standards. Influencer marketing is subject to regulations that vary by country, but common requirements include proper disclosure of sponsored content and adherence to advertising standards. It's the responsibility of both the brand and the influencer to ensure that these regulations are followed. This might involve adding hashtags like #ad or #sponsored to posts, or including a verbal disclosure in video content. Non-compliance can lead to penalties and damage to both the brand's and the influencer's reputation, so it's essential to take this aspect seriously.

After the campaign has been executed, the final step is to measure its success. This involves analyzing the campaign's performance against the goals you set at the beginning. Metrics to consider include reach, engagement, website traffic, conversion rates, and sales. It's important to look beyond vanity metrics, such as the number of likes or followers, and focus on the metrics that directly impact your business objectives. For instance, if the goal was to drive traffic to your website, then the number of click-throughs and time spent on the site will be more important than the number of likes on a post.

In addition to quantitative metrics, qualitative feedback is also valuable. This might include the sentiment of comments on social media, feedback from customers, or insights from the influencer about how the campaign was received by their audience. This feedback can provide context to the numbers and help you understand the broader impact of the campaign. It can also offer insights into what worked well and what could be improved in future campaigns.

Another important aspect of measuring success is understanding the long-term impact of the campaign. Influencer marketing is not always about immediate results; it can also have a lasting effect on brand awareness, reputation, and customer loyalty. For instance, a successful campaign might lead to an increase in followers on your brand's social media channels, or more mentions of your brand in conversations online. These long-term effects can be just as valuable, if not more so, than the immediate outcomes of the campaign.

Once the results have been analyzed, the final step is to document the campaign's learnings. This involves creating a report that summarizes the campaign's performance, highlights key takeaways, and provides recommendations for future campaigns. This report can serve as a valuable resource for your marketing team, helping to refine your influencer marketing strategy and improve future campaigns. It's also worth sharing this report with the influencer, as it can help them understand what worked well and where there might be opportunities for improvement.

In conclusion, creating effective influencer campaigns is a multifaceted process that requires careful planning, execution, and analysis. It's about more than just choosing the right influencers; it's about crafting a campaign that aligns with your brand's goals, resonates with your target audience, and leverages the unique strengths of the influencer. By focusing on these elements and maintaining a collaborative approach, you can create campaigns that not only achieve your immediate objectives but also contribute to the long-term success of your brand.

Chapter 4: Legal Considerations and Contracts

In the world of influencer marketing, where creativity and authenticity reign supreme, it can be easy to overlook the less glamorous aspects like legal considerations and contracts. However, these are crucial components that can make or break a campaign. Navigating the legal landscape of influencer marketing requires a solid understanding of the rules and regulations that govern advertising, as well as the ability to craft contracts that protect both the brand and the influencer. This chapter delves into the key legal issues and best practices for creating contracts that ensure a smooth and successful partnership.

One of the most important legal considerations in influencer marketing is disclosure. Governments and regulatory bodies across the globe have implemented strict guidelines to ensure that sponsored content is clearly identified as such. The Federal Trade Commission (FTC) in the United States, for instance, requires that influencers disclose any material connection they have with a brand when promoting products or services. This connection could be anything from receiving free products to being paid for a post. The purpose of these regulations is to protect consumers from being misled by undisclosed advertising.

For brands, ensuring compliance with these disclosure requirements is not just a legal obligation but also a matter of maintaining trust with the audience. Failure to comply can result in hefty fines, not to mention damage to both the brand's and the influencer's reputation. To avoid any issues, it's essential to make sure that influencers understand their disclosure obligations. This typically involves including clear guidelines in the contract about how disclosures should be made. For instance, the FTC recommends that disclosures be clear and conspicuous, using straightforward language like "#ad" or "#sponsored" at the beginning of a post or within the first few lines of a caption.

In addition to disclosure requirements, there are other legal aspects to consider when engaging in influencer marketing. Intellectual property rights, for example, play a significant role in the content created by influencers. When an influencer produces content for a brand, it's important to determine who owns that content and how it can be used. This is where contracts come into play. A well-drafted contract will specify whether the brand has the right to use the content beyond the initial post, such as in future marketing campaigns, on the brand's website, or in other promotional materials. It will also clarify whether the influencer retains any rights to the content, including the right to reuse it for other purposes.

Another important aspect of influencer contracts is exclusivity. Brands may want to ensure that the influencer does not promote competing products or services during the campaign period, or even for a certain time afterward. Exclusivity clauses can help protect the brand's investment by ensuring that the influencer's endorsement is seen as genuine and not diluted by conflicting messages. However, it's important to strike a balance, as overly restrictive exclusivity terms can deter influencers, especially those who work across multiple niches or industries. The terms of exclusivity should be reasonable and fair, reflecting the scope and nature of the partnership.

Payment terms are another critical element of influencer contracts. Influencers can be compensated in various ways, including flat fees, performance-based incentives, or product exchanges. Whatever the method, the contract should clearly outline the payment structure, including the amount, payment schedule, and any conditions that must be met before payment is released. For example, if the payment is contingent on the influencer achieving certain metrics, such as a specific number of views or clicks, these should be clearly defined and agreed upon by both parties. Clear payment terms help avoid misunderstandings and ensure that both the brand and the influencer are aligned on expectations.

In addition to these core elements, influencer contracts should also address other potential issues that could arise during the course of the partnership. For example, what happens if the influencer fails to deliver the content on time, or if the content does not meet the brand's standards? A well-drafted contract will include provisions for these scenarios, such as deadlines for content delivery, approval processes, and remedies for breaches of contract. It's also important to include clauses that protect the brand in case the influencer's conduct or actions negatively impact the brand's reputation. This could involve a morality clause, which allows the brand to terminate the contract if the influencer engages in behavior that is deemed unethical or damaging to the brand.

Another legal consideration in influencer marketing is compliance with data protection and privacy laws. With the rise of digital marketing, personal data has become a valuable asset, but it's also subject to stringent regulations. Brands that work with influencers may need to collect and process data related to the campaign, such as audience demographics, engagement metrics, or consumer feedback. It's essential to ensure that any data collected is handled in accordance with relevant data protection laws, such as the General Data Protection Regulation (GDPR) in the European Union. The contract should outline how data will be collected, stored, and used, and it should include provisions for safeguarding the influencer's and the audience's privacy.

Working with influencers also involves navigating the complexities of tax laws. Influencers who receive payment or products in exchange for their services are typically required to report this income to the tax authorities. Brands should ensure that they are complying with their own tax obligations, such as withholding taxes where applicable and providing the necessary tax documentation to the influencer. It's a good idea to consult with a tax professional to ensure that all parties are meeting their legal obligations and to avoid any surprises at tax time.

As influencer marketing continues to evolve, so too do the legal challenges associated with it. New platforms, technologies, and marketing strategies bring new legal considerations that brands and influencers must navigate. For instance, the rise of virtual influencers—digital avatars or AI-generated personas—raises questions about liability, intellectual property, and authenticity. Brands that choose to work with virtual influencers will need to consider how these unique characteristics impact their legal strategy and contracts.

In addition to keeping up with legal developments, brands should also be aware of industry best practices when it comes to influencer marketing. Many industry organizations, such as the Influencer Marketing Council or the American Marketing Association, provide guidelines and resources to help brands and influencers navigate the legal landscape. Staying informed about these best practices can help brands avoid common pitfalls and ensure that their influencer marketing campaigns are both legally compliant and ethically sound.

Ultimately, the goal of addressing legal considerations and contracts in influencer marketing is to create a solid foundation for the partnership. By clearly outlining the terms of the agreement, both the brand and the influencer can enter the relationship with a shared understanding of expectations, responsibilities, and rights. This not only helps to protect both parties from legal risks but also fosters a positive and productive working relationship.

While legal considerations and contracts might not be the most exciting aspect of influencer marketing, they are essential for ensuring the success of a campaign. Brands that take the time to understand and address these issues will be better equipped to navigate the complexities of influencer marketing and build lasting, mutually beneficial partnerships with influencers. Whether it's ensuring compliance with disclosure regulations, protecting intellectual property rights, or crafting fair and balanced contracts, these legal elements play a critical role in the overall success of an influencer marketing strategy.

By approaching legal considerations and contracts with the same care and attention to detail as the creative aspects of influencer marketing, brands can mitigate risks and set the stage for successful campaigns that not only achieve their marketing goals but also uphold the integrity and trustworthiness of both the brand and the influencer. This holistic approach to influencer marketing, where legal and creative elements are given equal importance, is key to building strong, lasting partnerships that drive real results.

Chapter 5: Measuring the ROI of Influencer Marketing

Measuring the return on investment (ROI) of influencer marketing is one of the most important, yet often challenging, aspects of running successful campaigns. While the allure of influencer marketing lies in its ability to create authentic connections and drive brand engagement, the true value of these efforts must be quantified to justify ongoing investment. This chapter delves into the methods and metrics used to measure the ROI of influencer marketing, offering a comprehensive guide to evaluating the effectiveness of your campaigns.

At its core, ROI in influencer marketing is about understanding the relationship between the resources invested in a campaign and the results it generates. Unlike traditional marketing channels where metrics like click-through rates or conversion rates are well established, influencer marketing requires a more nuanced approach. This is because influencer marketing is not just about direct sales; it's also about brand awareness, audience engagement, and long-term brand loyalty, all of which are more difficult to quantify but equally important to the overall success of a campaign.

The first step in measuring ROI is setting clear and measurable goals before the campaign begins. These goals should be directly tied to your overall marketing objectives and should guide the selection of influencers, the content strategy, and the metrics used to evaluate success. For instance, if your primary goal is to increase brand awareness, your ROI might be measured in terms of reach and impressions. On the other hand, if your goal is to drive sales, you'll be more focused on metrics like conversion rates and revenue generated from the campaign. Setting these goals upfront provides a clear framework for assessing the impact of your influencer marketing efforts.

Once your goals are defined, the next step is to identify the key performance indicators (KPIs) that will be used to measure success. These KPIs will vary depending on the nature of the campaign and the platform used, but common ones include reach, engagement, website traffic, conversions, and sales. Each of these metrics offers a different perspective on the campaign's performance, and together they provide a holistic view of its effectiveness.

Reach and impressions are often the first metrics brands look at when evaluating the success of an influencer campaign. These metrics indicate how many people have seen the content, which is crucial for brand awareness campaigns. However, while reach is important, it's not the be-all and end-all. High reach does not necessarily translate to high engagement or conversions, so it's important to look beyond these top-line numbers to understand the true impact of the campaign.

Engagement is another critical metric, and it offers deeper insights into how the audience is interacting with the content. Engagement metrics include likes, comments, shares, and saves on platforms like Instagram, retweets and replies on Twitter, and likes and comments on YouTube videos or TikTok posts. High engagement indicates that the content is resonating with the audience, which can be a strong indicator of brand affinity and interest. Furthermore, engagement can often be a predictor of future actions, such as website visits or purchases, making it a valuable metric for understanding the potential long-term impact of the campaign.

Website traffic is a direct and measurable way to see how an influencer campaign is driving potential customers to your site. This metric is particularly important for e-commerce brands or those looking to boost online sales. Tools like Google Analytics allow you to track the traffic that comes from specific influencers, enabling you to see which influencers are most effective at driving visitors to your site. Additionally, tracking metrics such as bounce rate, time on site, and pages per session can provide insights into the quality of the traffic generated by the campaign. If visitors are spending more time on your site and exploring multiple pages, it's a good sign that the influencer's content is not just attracting clicks, but also engaging potential customers.

Conversions and sales are the ultimate metrics for most influencer marketing campaigns, particularly those focused on driving revenue. Conversions can include a variety of actions depending on your goals, such as signing up for a newsletter, downloading a guide, or making a purchase. Tracking these actions allows you to directly attribute sales or leads to specific influencers or pieces of content. This can be done through tools like UTM parameters, which track the source of the traffic, or affiliate links that allow you to see exactly how many sales were generated by a particular influencer. Understanding the cost per conversion or the return on ad spend (ROAS) from influencer marketing can help you determine the financial viability of your campaigns and inform future budgeting decisions.

While these metrics are essential for understanding the quantitative impact of your influencer campaigns, it's also important to consider qualitative metrics that capture the broader impact on brand perception and customer sentiment. This can include analyzing the sentiment of comments on influencer posts, tracking brand mentions across social media, or conducting surveys to gauge customer opinions before and after the campaign. Qualitative feedback can provide valuable insights into how the campaign has affected brand awareness, customer loyalty, and overall brand sentiment. For example, if you see a surge in positive mentions of your brand or an increase in customer satisfaction scores, it's a strong indication that the influencer campaign has had a positive impact beyond just sales or traffic.

Another important aspect of measuring ROI in influencer marketing is understanding the long-term impact of your campaigns. While some campaigns may deliver immediate results in terms of sales or traffic, others may contribute to building brand equity over time. For instance, a campaign that significantly increases your social media following or improves your brand's reputation might not have an immediate impact on sales, but it can lead to greater customer loyalty and higher lifetime value in the long run. To capture this long-term impact, it's important to track metrics over time and compare the performance of customers acquired through influencer campaigns to those acquired through other channels.

Additionally, measuring the ROI of influencer marketing involves comparing the performance of different influencers and content types. Not all influencers or content will perform equally, and understanding what works best for your brand is key to optimizing future campaigns. This might involve A/B testing different types of content, such as video versus static images, or comparing the performance of micro-influencers versus macro-influencers. By analyzing the data, you can identify trends and patterns that can inform your influencer strategy, helping you allocate your budget more effectively and achieve better results in the future.

Another layer to consider is the platform on which the campaign is executed. Different social media platforms have varying strengths and user demographics, which can affect the performance of an influencer campaign. For example, Instagram is known for its high engagement rates and is often used for visual storytelling, making it ideal for lifestyle and fashion brands. On the other hand, YouTube is better suited for in-depth product reviews or tutorials, which can drive higher conversions for tech or beauty brands. Understanding the nuances of each platform and how they align with your brand and audience is crucial for maximizing ROI.

Collaboration and feedback loops with influencers are also critical to improving the ROI of future campaigns. Influencers often have deep insights into their audience's preferences and behaviors, which can be invaluable for refining your strategy. By maintaining open communication with influencers and involving them in the analysis process, you can gain a better understanding of what worked and what didn't. This collaborative approach not only strengthens the relationship with the influencer but also ensures that future campaigns are more effective and aligned with audience expectations.

Finally, it's important to contextualize the ROI of influencer marketing within your overall marketing strategy. Influencer marketing should not be viewed in isolation but as part of a broader, integrated marketing approach. Comparing the ROI of influencer marketing with other channels, such as paid search or email marketing, can provide insights into its relative effectiveness and help you allocate your marketing budget more efficiently. For instance, if influencer marketing consistently delivers a higher ROI than other channels, it may be worth increasing your investment in influencer campaigns. Conversely, if the ROI is lower, you might need to adjust your strategy or focus on optimizing other channels.

In summary, measuring the ROI of influencer marketing is a complex but essential task for ensuring the success of your campaigns. By setting clear goals, identifying relevant KPIs, and using a combination of quantitative and qualitative metrics, you can gain a comprehensive understanding of the impact of your influencer marketing efforts. Furthermore, by analyzing the performance of different influencers, content types, and platforms, you can optimize your strategy for future campaigns and maximize your return on investment. Whether your goal is to drive sales, increase brand awareness, or build long-term customer loyalty, measuring ROI is the key to unlocking the full potential of influencer marketing and ensuring that your efforts deliver real, measurable results.

Chapter 6: Micro-Influencers vs. Macro-Influencers

In the evolving landscape of influencer marketing, one of the most crucial decisions brands face is choosing between micro-influencers and macro-influencers. Both categories offer unique advantages, and the choice between them can significantly impact the success of a campaign. Understanding the differences, strengths, and potential drawbacks of each type of influencer is essential for crafting a strategy that aligns with your brand's goals and resonates with your target audience.

Micro-influencers are typically defined as individuals with a smaller but highly engaged following, often ranging from 1,000 to 100,000 followers. These influencers are usually niche-specific, with content that focuses on particular interests, hobbies, or lifestyles. The appeal of micro-influencers lies in their authenticity and close-knit relationships with their followers. Because they cater to a more focused audience, their recommendations often feel more personal and trustworthy, which can lead to higher engagement rates and, potentially, more effective conversions.

One of the key strengths of micro-influencers is their ability to cultivate strong bonds with their audience. Unlike macro-influencers, who might have millions of followers, micro-influencers tend to know their followers better and interact with them more frequently. This level of engagement fosters a sense of community, where followers feel like they are part of an exclusive group. This intimacy can be a powerful tool for brands, especially those looking to tap into specific niches or communities. When a micro-influencer endorses a product, it often feels like a recommendation from a trusted friend, which can be far more compelling than a mass-market advertisement.

Moreover, micro-influencers are often perceived as more relatable and authentic than their macro counterparts. They are usually individuals who have grown their following organically by sharing genuine content that reflects their real lives, rather than polished, high-production posts. This authenticity is a significant draw for consumers, particularly in an era where audiences are increasingly skeptical of overtly commercial content. Brands that collaborate with micro-influencers can benefit from this authenticity, as the endorsement is likely to be seen as more genuine and less like traditional advertising.

Another advantage of working with micro-influencers is cost-effectiveness. Because they have smaller followings, micro-influencers generally charge less for their services compared to macro-influencers. This makes them an attractive option for brands with limited budgets or those looking to run multiple campaigns simultaneously. Additionally, the lower cost allows brands to experiment with different influencers, content types, and strategies without the significant financial risk that comes with partnering with a single macro-influencer. This flexibility can be particularly beneficial for brands that are new to influencer marketing and want to test the waters before making a larger investment.

On the other hand, macro-influencers are individuals with a large following, typically in the hundreds of thousands or millions. These influencers often have a broader reach and can amplify a brand's message to a much larger audience. For brands looking to build widespread awareness or make a big splash with a campaign, macro-influencers can be a powerful asset. Their extensive reach means that even a single post can generate significant visibility, making them an ideal choice for campaigns aimed at mass-market appeal.

The scale of macro-influencers also means that they often have a higher level of professional polish in their content. Many macro-influencers treat their social media presence as a full-time job, investing in high-quality photography, video production, and editorial standards. This level of professionalism can be particularly appealing for brands that want to align themselves with a certain level of prestige or sophistication. A well-executed post from a macro-influencer can have the look and feel of a high-end advertisement, which can elevate the perceived value of the brand and attract attention from a broader audience.

However, working with macro-influencers comes with its own set of challenges. One of the main drawbacks is the cost. Due to their extensive reach and influence, macro-influencers command higher fees, which can be prohibitive for smaller brands or those with limited marketing budgets. Additionally, the large followings of macro-influencers often mean that their audiences are more diverse and less targeted than those of micro-influencers. While this broad reach can be advantageous for brand awareness, it may not translate into the same level of engagement or conversion as a more targeted campaign with micro-influencers.

Another potential downside of working with macro-influencers is the risk of perceived inauthenticity. As influencers grow their followings and attract more brand partnerships, their content can start to feel more commercialized. Followers might begin to question the authenticity of their endorsements, wondering whether they are driven by genuine affinity for the product or simply by the paycheck. This can lead to skepticism among the audience and diminish the impact of the campaign. Brands need to carefully consider the influencer's past collaborations and the tone of their content to ensure that the partnership will come across as credible.

When deciding between micro-influencers and macro-influencers, it's essential to consider the specific goals of the campaign. For example, if the objective is to drive immediate sales or conversions within a particular niche, micro-influencers might be the better choice due to their strong engagement and targeted audience. Their endorsements are likely to feel more personal and relevant, which can lead to higher conversion rates. Additionally, partnering with multiple micro-influencers across different niches can help brands reach diverse segments of their target market, each with a tailored message that resonates with that specific audience.

Conversely, if the goal is to create broad brand awareness or launch a new product to a wide audience, macro-influencers may offer the scale needed to achieve those objectives. Their ability to reach millions of followers with a single post can generate significant buzz and visibility, which is particularly valuable for major product launches, brand repositions, or campaigns designed to reach a broad demographic. In these cases, the sheer reach of a macro-influencer can be a critical factor in the campaign's success.

It's also worth considering the potential for hybrid strategies that combine the strengths of both micro and macro-influencers. For instance, a campaign could start with a macro-influencer to generate initial awareness and then follow up with a series of micro-influencer posts to sustain engagement and drive conversions. This approach allows brands to leverage the broad reach of a macro-influencer while still benefiting from the authenticity and targeted engagement of micro-influencers. Additionally, hybrid strategies can provide more touchpoints for the audience, increasing the likelihood that the message will resonate and stick.

The choice between micro and macro-influencers is not a one-size-fits-all decision; it requires a nuanced understanding of the brand's goals, the target audience, and the dynamics of the specific market. It's also important to recognize that the influencer landscape is continually evolving, with new trends, platforms, and types of influencers emerging all the time. For example, the rise of nano-influencers—those with fewer than 10,000 followers—has introduced another layer of complexity to influencer marketing strategies. These influencers often have even more intimate connections with their followers, offering brands the potential for hyper-targeted campaigns that feel incredibly personal and authentic.

In the end, the effectiveness of an influencer campaign hinges on more than just the size of the influencer's following. It's about choosing the right influencers for your brand, understanding their audience, and crafting a campaign that leverages their unique strengths. Whether you opt for micro, macro, or a combination of both, the key is to ensure that the content feels authentic, resonates with the audience, and aligns with your brand's overall strategy.

As influencer marketing continues to grow and evolve, the distinctions between micro and macro-influencers may become less rigid, with more brands recognizing the value of a balanced approach that takes advantage of the strengths of both. By staying attuned to these trends and continuously evaluating the performance of your campaigns, you can make informed decisions that maximize the impact of your influencer marketing efforts. Ultimately, whether you're working with micro-influencers to build deep connections within a niche community or leveraging the broad reach of a macro-influencer to amplify your message, the goal remains the same: to create meaningful, engaging, and effective content that drives results for your brand.

Chapter 7: Influencer Marketing on Different Platforms

Influencer marketing is a dynamic field, and much of its success hinges on choosing the right platforms to engage with your target audience. Different social media platforms offer distinct opportunities and challenges for influencer marketing, each with its own user demographics, content formats, and engagement styles. Understanding the nuances of these platforms is crucial for crafting campaigns that not only reach your audience but also resonate with them in meaningful ways. This chapter explores the major social media platforms used in influencer marketing, analyzing their strengths and how brands can effectively leverage them.

Instagram is often seen as the cornerstone of influencer marketing, and for good reason. It's a visually-driven platform that lends itself well to lifestyle content, making it ideal for brands in fashion, beauty, travel, and food. Instagram's features, such as Stories, Reels, and the Shop tab, offer multiple avenues for influencers to showcase products and for followers to engage with them. The platform's algorithm favors content that receives high engagement, which can amplify the reach of influencer posts. Furthermore, Instagram's audience tends to skew younger, with a large proportion of users falling in the 18-34 age range, making it particularly effective for brands targeting Millennials and Gen Z.

One of Instagram's key strengths is its visual nature, which allows influencers to create aesthetically pleasing content that aligns with a brand's image. High-quality images, short-form videos, and interactive content like polls or quizzes in Stories can all be used to capture attention and foster engagement. The platform's focus on visuals also means that the influencer's personal style plays a significant role in the effectiveness of the campaign. Brands that work with influencers who have a distinct aesthetic that complements their products are likely to see better results.

Instagram Stories have become a powerful tool for influencer marketing, offering a more casual and ephemeral way to share content. Stories allow influencers to give followers a behind-the-scenes look at their lives, share quick updates, or promote products in a way that feels spontaneous and authentic. The swipe-up feature (available to influencers with over 10,000 followers) is particularly valuable for driving traffic to external websites, making it an excellent tool for e-commerce brands. Additionally, Instagram's Shopping feature allows users to purchase products directly through the app, streamlining the path from discovery to purchase and making the platform a powerful driver of sales.

Instagram Reels, the platform's answer to TikTok, provides another avenue for creative expression and engagement. Reels are short, engaging videos that can go viral quickly due to Instagram's algorithmic push for this content format. They're particularly effective for trends, challenges, and showcasing products in a fun, dynamic way. Brands that can tap into the creativity of Reels while aligning with an influencer's style can create content that not only reaches a broad audience but also feels fresh and relevant.

While Instagram is a powerhouse, TikTok has emerged as a game-changer in the influencer marketing space. Known for its short-form, highly engaging video content, TikTok has become a cultural phenomenon, particularly among Gen Z. The platform's algorithm is unique in that it prioritizes content discovery over follower count, meaning that even accounts with relatively few followers can achieve viral success. This democratization of content has led to the rise of many new influencers, who can gain massive followings in a short period based on the virality of their videos.

TikTok's content is driven by creativity, humor, and authenticity, making it a fertile ground for influencer marketing. Brands that collaborate with influencers on TikTok often see success when they allow the influencer to have creative freedom, as the platform's audience values originality and spontaneity. Whether it's participating in trending challenges, creating branded hashtag campaigns, or sharing product tutorials in a unique way, TikTok influencers have a knack for making content that resonates with their followers while subtly integrating brand messaging.

One of TikTok's most significant advantages is its potential for virality. The platform's For You page, which curates content for users based on their interests and behavior, can propel a video to millions of views in a matter of hours. This kind of exposure is invaluable for brands looking to create buzz around a new product or campaign. However, the ephemeral nature of TikTok content also means that trends and user interests can shift rapidly, so brands need to be agile and ready to capitalize on opportunities as they arise.

YouTube remains a dominant platform for long-form video content and is particularly effective for in-depth product reviews, tutorials, and unboxing videos. The platform's audience is diverse, spanning various age groups and interests, making it suitable for a wide range of brands. YouTube influencers, or "YouTubers," have built loyal followings through consistent content creation and often have a deep connection with their audience, which can translate into high trust and influence when they recommend products.

One of YouTube's strengths lies in its ability to accommodate detailed and informative content. This makes it an ideal platform for brands that require a more thorough exploration of their products. For instance, beauty brands can benefit from detailed makeup tutorials, while tech companies might find success with influencers who create comprehensive reviews and unboxing videos. The longer format also allows for more nuanced storytelling, enabling influencers to weave brand messages into content in a way that feels organic and informative rather than overtly promotional.

YouTube's monetization features, such as AdSense and memberships, also incentivize influencers to create content that aligns with their brand partnerships. Sponsored content on YouTube often takes the form of integrated ads, where influencers incorporate brand messages into their videos seamlessly. This approach can be highly effective, as it leverages the trust and rapport that influencers have built with their audience over time. Furthermore, the platform's searchability means that content can have a long shelf life, continuing to generate views and engagement long after the initial post.

Twitter, while not as visually driven as Instagram or TikTok, remains an important platform for influencer marketing, particularly for brands looking to engage in real-time conversations or tap into trending topics. Twitter influencers, often referred to as "tastemakers," are known for their ability to drive discussions, share insights, and influence public opinion. The platform's fast-paced nature makes it ideal for brands that want to stay on the pulse of cultural moments or engage with their audience in a more conversational manner.

Twitter's strength lies in its ability to facilitate direct interaction between brands, influencers, and consumers. Influencers on Twitter often engage in dialogue with their followers, respond to questions, and share personal opinions, making their endorsements feel more like genuine recommendations rather than advertisements. Brands can leverage this by participating in Twitter chats, creating branded hashtags, or collaborating with influencers to launch Twitter-based campaigns. Additionally, Twitter's use of threads allows influencers to share more detailed narratives or information, which can be particularly useful for educational content or storytelling.

Facebook, while often perceived as a platform for older demographics, still holds significant value in the influencer marketing landscape. With its diverse user base and robust advertising tools, Facebook offers a comprehensive ecosystem for influencer campaigns. Facebook Groups, in particular, have become a powerful tool for niche communities, where influencers can engage with highly targeted audiences in a more intimate setting. These groups often revolve around shared interests, making them fertile ground for brands to build deeper connections with consumers.

Facebook's strengths also lie in its ability to integrate various content types, including text, images, videos, and live streams. This versatility allows influencers to create a rich tapestry of content that can cater to different segments of their audience. Live streaming, in particular, has gained traction on Facebook, with influencers using it to host Q&A sessions, product demonstrations, or behind-the-scenes glimpses. This real-time interaction can create a sense of immediacy and connection, enhancing the impact of the influencer's endorsement.

Pinterest is another platform that, while often overlooked, can be a powerful tool for influencer marketing, especially for brands in the lifestyle, DIY, and e-commerce sectors. Pinterest is a visual discovery engine where users search for inspiration, ideas, and products. Influencers on Pinterest, known as "Pinners," create and curate boards that showcase products, DIY projects, recipes, and more. The platform's focus on visual discovery makes it an excellent fit for brands that want to reach users who are in the planning or decision-making phase of their purchasing journey.

Pinterest's unique selling point is its ability to drive long-term traffic. Unlike other platforms where content is quickly consumed and forgotten, pins on Pinterest can resurface and gain traction months or even years after they are first posted. This long-term visibility makes Pinterest a valuable platform for evergreen content that continues to drive traffic and sales over time. Brands can collaborate with influencers to create pins that highlight products, link back to e-commerce sites, or provide value through tutorials and guides.

LinkedIn, while primarily known as a professional networking platform, has also become a viable channel for influencer marketing, particularly for B2B brands. LinkedIn influencers, often industry experts or thought leaders, have the ability to influence business decisions and shape professional conversations. Brands looking to establish thought leadership, share industry insights, or promote professional services can benefit from collaborating with LinkedIn influencers. The platform's focus on professional content also means that influencer campaigns on LinkedIn tend to be more formal and informative, catering to an audience that values expertise and credibility.

Each platform offers unique advantages and caters to different types of content and audiences. The key to successful influencer marketing lies in understanding these nuances and aligning your campaign strategy with the strengths of the chosen platform. By doing so, brands can create more targeted, engaging, and effective influencer campaigns that resonate with their audience and achieve their marketing goals. Whether it's the visual allure of Instagram, the viral potential of TikTok, the depth of YouTube, the conversational nature of Twitter, the community focus of Facebook, the discovery engine of Pinterest, or the professional credibility of LinkedIn, each platform offers a distinct pathway to reach and influence consumers in the digital age.

Chapter 8: Case Studies of Successful Influencer Campaigns

Successful influencer marketing campaigns are as much about strategy as they are about creativity. The best campaigns manage to strike a balance between the influencer's authentic voice and the brand's messaging, creating content that resonates with audiences and drives measurable results. To understand what makes these campaigns effective, it's helpful to look at some standout examples where brands have leveraged influencers to achieve their goals. These case studies illustrate how different approaches, when executed well, can lead to significant success.

One of the most iconic influencer marketing campaigns in recent years is Glossier's approach to building a beauty empire. Glossier, a skincare and beauty brand, was founded on the principle of community-driven product development. Rather than relying solely on traditional advertising, Glossier tapped into the power of micro-influencers and regular customers who genuinely loved their products. The brand built its reputation by engaging with beauty enthusiasts who had modest but highly engaged followings. These individuals weren't celebrities or professional influencers at the outset; they were everyday people who shared their beauty routines on social media.

Glossier's strategy was simple yet effective: they empowered their customers to become brand ambassadors. By sharing user-generated content, reposting customer reviews, and encouraging their followers to share their experiences with Glossier products, the brand created a grassroots movement. This approach not only built trust among consumers but also fostered a sense of community around the brand. The results were impressive—Glossier grew rapidly, gaining a loyal customer base that felt personally connected to the brand's ethos. The key takeaway from Glossier's success is the power of authenticity and community. By focusing on real people with real experiences, Glossier was able to build a brand that resonated deeply with its audience.

Another standout campaign is the collaboration between Nike and Colin Kaepernick. Nike's decision to feature the controversial former NFL quarterback in their "Just Do It" campaign was a bold move that generated widespread attention. Kaepernick had gained national attention for kneeling during the national anthem as a protest against racial injustice, making him a polarizing figure. Nike's decision to align with Kaepernick sent a powerful message about the brand's values, sparking conversations and debates across the country.

The campaign was highly effective because it tapped into a broader cultural moment and positioned Nike as a brand that wasn't afraid to take a stand on important social issues. The hashtag #JustDoIt trended globally, and the campaign garnered millions of impressions across social media platforms. Despite initial backlash from some consumers, Nike's stock surged, and the campaign was ultimately credited with strengthening the brand's connection with its core audience—young, diverse, and socially conscious consumers. The success of this campaign highlights the importance of aligning your brand with influencers who embody your values, even if it means taking risks.

Moving to the food and beverage industry, one cannot overlook the success of Pepsi's partnership with Kendall Jenner. While this campaign, which featured Jenner in a controversial advertisement, was widely criticized and ultimately pulled, it serves as a critical lesson in influencer marketing. The ad was intended to convey a message of unity and peace, with Jenner handing a police officer a can of Pepsi during a protest. However, it was met with significant backlash for trivializing serious social issues and appropriating protest movements for commercial gain.

The campaign's failure underscores the importance of sensitivity and awareness when creating influencer content, particularly when it touches on social or political themes. It's a reminder that while influencers can bring significant attention to a brand, the messaging must be handled with care. Missteps can lead to negative publicity and damage to the brand's reputation, as was the case with Pepsi. This campaign demonstrates the need for brands to thoroughly vet their creative concepts and consider the potential reactions from diverse audiences.

On a more positive note, Airbnb's "Live There" campaign is a textbook example of how to leverage influencers to enhance brand storytelling. Airbnb partnered with a diverse group of influencers, including photographers, travel bloggers, and digital nomads, to showcase the unique experiences that staying in an Airbnb property can offer. Rather than simply promoting the properties, the campaign focused on the idea of living like a local—immersing oneself in the culture and community of the destination.

The influencers shared their personal stories and experiences, creating content that was both visually stunning and emotionally engaging. This approach resonated with travelers who were looking for more than just a place to stay—they wanted an authentic, immersive experience. The campaign was successful in positioning Airbnb as a brand that offers more than just accommodations; it's a gateway to unique, memorable travel experiences. The "Live There" campaign demonstrates the effectiveness of using influencer marketing to tell a broader brand story, one that goes beyond the product and taps into the aspirations and desires of the audience.

In the fashion industry, the collaboration between Daniel Wellington and a wide array of influencers is a prime example of scaling influencer marketing effectively. Daniel Wellington, a Swedish watch brand, built its entire marketing strategy around influencers. The brand targeted Instagram influencers, offering them free watches in exchange for posts featuring the product along with a personalized discount code. This strategy allowed Daniel Wellington to reach millions of potential customers through a network of influencers who ranged from micro to macro.

What made this campaign particularly successful was its scalability and consistency. The influencers, regardless of their follower count, shared similar types of content that aligned with the brand's minimalist aesthetic. This created a cohesive brand image across social media, making Daniel Wellington watches instantly recognizable. The use of discount codes not only incentivized followers to purchase but also allowed the brand to track the effectiveness of each influencer partnership. As a result, Daniel Wellington saw exponential growth in both brand awareness and sales, proving that a well-executed influencer strategy can serve as the backbone of a brand's marketing efforts.

Another noteworthy example is the partnership between the video game company EA Sports and various YouTube and Twitch influencers for the launch of FIFA games. EA Sports leveraged the massive followings of gaming influencers who specialize in sports games to create excitement and anticipation for new FIFA releases. These influencers streamed gameplay, participated in challenges, and shared tips and tricks, all while promoting the game.

The success of these campaigns lies in the deep engagement that gaming influencers have with their audiences. Fans of these influencers trust their opinions and are highly likely to follow their recommendations. By integrating the game into content that the audience was already passionate about, EA Sports was able to generate buzz and drive pre-orders and sales. The campaign also highlighted the importance of choosing influencers who are not only popular but also relevant to the product. In the case of FIFA, partnering with influencers who were genuinely enthusiastic about the game helped create authentic content that resonated with the gaming community.

In the beauty industry, the collaboration between Morphe and James Charles stands out as a significant success. James Charles, a beauty influencer with a massive following, partnered with Morphe to create the James Charles Artistry Palette, a collection of vibrant eyeshadows. The collaboration was not just about slapping a name on a product; Charles was deeply involved in the development of the palette, from selecting the colors to designing the packaging.

The campaign was a massive success, with the palette selling out within minutes of its launch. Charles's followers, who had a deep connection with him and trusted his expertise, were eager to purchase a product that he had personally endorsed and helped create. The success of this campaign illustrates the power of influencer collaborations that go beyond simple endorsements. By involving the influencer in the product development process, Morphe was able to create a product that felt authentic and personal, which in turn drove strong sales and solidified the brand's position in the beauty industry.

The fitness brand Gymshark also provides an excellent case study in how to build a brand using influencer marketing. Gymshark started as a small startup selling fitness apparel and quickly grew into a global brand by partnering with fitness influencers on Instagram and YouTube. The brand focused on influencers who embodied the Gymshark ethos of hard work, dedication, and a passion for fitness. These influencers shared workout routines, fitness tips, and motivational content while wearing Gymshark apparel, creating a strong association between the brand and the fitness lifestyle.

Gymshark's strategy was to create a community around the brand, where influencers and their followers felt like they were part of something bigger. The brand organized events, meetups, and collaborations that further strengthened this sense of community. This approach paid off, as Gymshark's influencer-driven marketing strategy helped the brand achieve massive growth and establish itself as a leader in the fitness industry. The success of

Gymshark demonstrates the power of building a brand community through influencer marketing, where the brand becomes synonymous with a particular lifestyle or mindset.

These case studies highlight the diversity of approaches in influencer marketing, from grassroots campaigns with micro-influencers to high-profile partnerships with celebrities and macro-influencers. What they all have in common is a focus on authenticity, relevance, and strategic alignment between the brand and the influencer. By carefully selecting influencers who align with their brand values and crafting campaigns that resonate with their target audience, these brands were able to achieve significant success and, in many cases, redefine their industries.

Whether it's leveraging the power of community, tapping into cultural moments, or co-creating products with influencers, these examples offer valuable lessons for brands looking to harness the potential of influencer marketing. The key is to approach each campaign with a clear understanding of the brand's goals, the influencer's audience, and the broader cultural context, ensuring that the partnership feels authentic and delivers real value to both the brand and the consumer.

Chapter 9: The Future of Influencer Marketing

The future of influencer marketing is evolving rapidly, driven by changes in technology, consumer behavior, and the social media landscape. What began as a novel way for brands to reach audiences through trusted voices has now become a sophisticated and multifaceted industry. As influencer marketing continues to mature, brands and influencers alike must adapt to new trends and challenges to stay relevant and effective. This chapter explores the key trends shaping the future of influencer marketing, offering insights into where the industry is headed and how brands can prepare for what's next.

One of the most significant shifts in influencer marketing is the increasing emphasis on authenticity and transparency. As consumers become more savvy and discerning, they demand more genuine interactions with brands and influencers. The days of blatant product placements and overly promotional content are fading. Audiences are seeking out influencers who share their values and interests, and who promote products in a way that feels natural and trustworthy. This shift has led to a rise in influencers who are selective about the brands they work with, choosing partnerships that align with their personal brand and resonate with their audience.

To maintain this level of authenticity, influencers are now more involved in the creative process, often collaborating with brands to co-create content that feels organic. This approach not only enhances the credibility of the influencer's endorsement but also allows for more innovative and engaging campaigns. For brands, this means moving away from rigid, one-size-fits-all briefs and towards more flexible, collaborative partnerships where influencers have a say in how the brand is presented. This trend is likely to continue as brands realize that the most effective influencer marketing is built on trust and mutual respect.

Another major trend shaping the future of influencer marketing is the rise of niche influencers. While mega-influencers and celebrities with millions of followers will always have their place, there is a growing recognition of the power of micro-influencers and nano-influencers. These influencers, who typically have smaller but highly engaged followings, are becoming increasingly valuable to brands. Their audiences are often more targeted and loyal, which can lead to higher engagement rates and more meaningful interactions.

Niche influencers offer brands the opportunity to reach specific segments of their target market in a way that feels personal and relevant. Whether it's a beauty influencer who specializes in cruelty-free products or a fitness enthusiast who focuses on sustainable living, these influencers bring a depth of knowledge and passion to their content that resonates with like-minded followers. For brands, partnering with niche influencers can lead to more effective campaigns that drive real results, particularly in areas like conversions and customer loyalty.

As the influencer landscape becomes more specialized, we're also seeing a shift towards long-term partnerships rather than one-off campaigns. Brands are increasingly recognizing the value of building ongoing relationships with influencers, rather than treating them as temporary spokespeople. Long-term collaborations allow influencers to become true ambassadors for a brand, with a deeper understanding of its values, products, and goals. This, in turn, enables influencers to create more authentic and consistent content, which strengthens the bond with their audience over time.

These long-term partnerships are beneficial for both brands and influencers. For brands, they offer a more stable and predictable marketing strategy, with influencers who are genuinely invested in the brand's success. For influencers, long-term collaborations provide financial stability and the opportunity to develop a deeper relationship with their followers around the brand. This trend is likely to grow as both parties realize that consistency and authenticity are key to sustaining audience trust and driving long-term growth.

The future of influencer marketing is also being shaped by advances in technology, particularly the rise of artificial intelligence (AI) and machine learning. AI is already playing a significant role in the way brands identify and select influencers, analyze campaign performance, and optimize content. Influencer marketing platforms are using AI to sift through vast amounts of data to identify the most relevant influencers based on factors like audience demographics, engagement rates, and content style. This technology allows brands to make more informed decisions about which influencers to work with, leading to more targeted and effective campaigns.

AI is also being used to create virtual influencers—computer-generated characters that are designed to engage with audiences on social media. These virtual influencers can be tailored to fit a brand's specific needs, from their appearance to their personality and interests. While the idea of virtual influencers might seem far-fetched, they are already being used by some brands with significant success. Virtual influencers offer a level of control and consistency that human influencers can't match, and they can be programmed to interact with followers in real-time, 24/7. However, the use of virtual influencers raises questions about authenticity and the human connection that is central to influencer marketing. As this technology evolves, it will be interesting to see how brands balance the benefits of virtual influencers with the need for genuine, human interactions.

Another technological advancement impacting influencer marketing is the growing importance of video content, particularly short-form video. Platforms like TikTok, Instagram Reels, and YouTube Shorts have exploded in popularity, driven by their ability to capture attention quickly and engage users with dynamic, entertaining content. Video content is highly engaging and often more effective at conveying a brand's message than static images or text. As a result, influencers are increasingly focusing on video as their primary content format, and brands are investing more in video-based campaigns.

The shift towards video content is also being driven by changes in consumer behavior. Audiences today are consuming more video than ever before, and they expect content to be entertaining, informative, and easily digestible. This has led to the rise of snackable content—short, bite-sized videos that are perfect for on-the-go consumption. For brands, this means creating content that is visually compelling and delivers a clear message within a matter of seconds. Influencers who are skilled at producing high-quality video content are likely to be in high demand as this trend continues.

Live streaming is another video trend that is gaining traction in the influencer marketing space. Platforms like Instagram Live, YouTube Live, and Twitch allow influencers to engage with their audience in real-time, creating a sense of immediacy and intimacy that is difficult to replicate with pre-recorded content. Live streams are particularly effective for product launches, Q&A sessions, and behind-the-scenes content, as they allow influencers to interact directly with their followers and respond to their questions and comments on the spot. For brands, live streaming offers a unique opportunity to create a two-way dialogue with consumers, fostering a deeper connection and driving real-time engagement.

In addition to technological advancements, the future of influencer marketing is being shaped by evolving consumer expectations around social responsibility and ethical marketing. Today's consumers are increasingly looking to brands to take a stand on social and environmental issues, and they expect influencers to do the same. This shift has given rise to a new wave of influencers who are not only content creators but also advocates for causes they are passionate about. These purpose-driven influencers use their platforms to raise awareness about issues such as climate change, social justice, and mental health, often partnering with brands that share their values.

For brands, working with purpose-driven influencers can be a powerful way to connect with socially conscious consumers. However, it's important that these partnerships are authentic and not seen as tokenistic or opportunistic. Consumers are quick to call out brands that engage in "woke-washing," where social or environmental causes are used as a marketing ploy without any real commitment to change. To avoid this, brands must ensure that their actions align with their messaging and that their partnerships with influencers are based on genuine shared values.

As influencer marketing continues to evolve, brands will need to stay ahead of the curve by embracing new trends, technologies, and consumer expectations. This will require a shift towards more strategic, data-driven approaches, where technology is leveraged to enhance the effectiveness of campaigns while maintaining the human connection that is at the heart of influencer marketing. It will also require a commitment to authenticity, transparency, and social responsibility, as consumers increasingly seek out brands and influencers that align with their values.

In the end, the future of influencer marketing will be defined by its ability to adapt to change. The industry has come a long way from its early days of simple product placements and paid posts, and it continues to evolve at a rapid pace. As new platforms emerge, technologies advance, and consumer behaviors shift, influencer marketing will remain a powerful tool for brands to connect with audiences in meaningful and impactful ways. By staying attuned to these changes and being willing to innovate, brands can ensure that their influencer marketing efforts remain relevant, effective, and truly influential in the years to come.

Chapter 10: Navigating Challenges in Influencer Marketing

Influencer marketing, despite its proven effectiveness, is not without its challenges. As brands continue to integrate influencer strategies into their broader marketing plans, they must also navigate a range of obstacles that can complicate campaign execution and impact results. These challenges can arise from various areas, including influencer selection, content authenticity, legal and regulatory compliance, and evolving consumer expectations. Understanding these challenges and developing strategies to address them is essential for brands seeking to maximize the effectiveness of their influencer marketing efforts.

One of the most significant challenges in influencer marketing is selecting the right influencers to represent a brand. While it might seem straightforward to choose influencers based on follower count or visibility, these metrics alone do not guarantee success. A high number of followers doesn't necessarily equate to high engagement or conversions. Brands must dig deeper to assess an influencer's audience demographics, engagement rates, content style, and overall alignment with brand values. Misalignment between the brand and the influencer can lead to inauthentic content, which can quickly be recognized by savvy consumers, resulting in diminished trust and effectiveness of the campaign.

To navigate this challenge, brands must invest time in thoroughly researching potential influencers. This involves not only analyzing their social media metrics but also understanding their audience's behavior and interests. Tools and platforms that offer detailed analytics can be invaluable in this process, providing insights into the influencer's reach, the authenticity of their following, and the type of content that resonates most with their audience. By focusing on engagement over sheer follower numbers, brands can identify influencers who truly connect with their audience and are more likely to drive meaningful results.

Another challenge is ensuring content authenticity in influencer partnerships. As influencer marketing has grown, so has consumer skepticism towards sponsored content. Audiences are increasingly wary of posts that feel overly commercial or disingenuous. This skepticism can undermine the impact of a campaign if consumers perceive that the influencer is simply promoting products for the sake of a paycheck, rather than out of genuine interest or belief in the product.

To combat this, brands must work closely with influencers to develop content that feels natural and aligns with the influencer's usual tone and style. This might mean giving influencers more creative freedom to integrate the brand message in a way that suits their content, rather than imposing rigid guidelines that lead to formulaic posts. Brands should aim to build long-term relationships with influencers, where the influencer genuinely becomes an advocate for the brand over time. This long-term approach not only fosters authenticity but also builds trust with the audience, as they see the influencer's endorsement as part of an ongoing relationship rather than a one-time transaction.

Legal and regulatory compliance is another area where brands can face significant challenges in influencer marketing. As the industry has grown, so too has the scrutiny from regulatory bodies like the Federal Trade Commission (FTC) in the United States and similar organizations worldwide. These regulators have established guidelines to ensure that influencer marketing practices are transparent and that consumers are not misled by undisclosed sponsored content. Failure to comply with these regulations can result in legal penalties for both the brand and the influencer, as well as damage to their reputations.

Navigating these legal requirements requires brands to stay informed about the latest regulations and to ensure that their influencer contracts include clear provisions about disclosure. Influencers should be required to disclose their relationships with brands in a manner that is clear and conspicuous, such as using hashtags like #ad or #sponsored at the beginning of a post. Additionally, brands should provide influencers with guidelines on how to comply with these regulations, while also monitoring content to ensure that these guidelines are being followed. Regular audits of influencer content can help brands catch any compliance issues early and address them before they escalate into larger problems.

Another significant challenge in influencer marketing is managing the expectations of both the brand and the influencer. Brands may have specific goals they want to achieve through influencer partnerships, such as increasing brand awareness, driving traffic, or boosting sales. However, these goals need to be realistic and aligned with the influencer's capabilities and audience. Mismatched expectations can lead to dissatisfaction on both sides, with the brand feeling that the campaign did not deliver the desired results, and the influencer feeling pressured to meet unrealistic demands.

To avoid this, brands should establish clear, measurable objectives from the outset and communicate these to the influencer. This might include setting specific KPIs, such as the number of impressions, engagement rates, or conversions expected from the campaign. It's also important for brands to be open to feedback from influencers, who may have valuable insights into what will resonate with their audience. By working together to set realistic goals and expectations, brands and influencers can collaborate more effectively and achieve mutually beneficial outcomes.

The fast-paced nature of social media also presents challenges in influencer marketing. Trends can change rapidly, and what resonates with audiences today may not work tomorrow. This fluid environment requires brands to be agile and ready to adapt their strategies on the fly. However, the need for speed can sometimes clash with the brand's desire for control, leading to tension in the creative process.

To manage this, brands need to strike a balance between planning and flexibility. While it's important to have a clear strategy and objectives, it's equally important to remain open to changes and to trust the influencer's judgment. Influencers are often more in tune with the latest trends and audience preferences, and their ability to pivot quickly can be a valuable asset. By building trust and maintaining open lines of communication, brands can empower influencers to take the lead in adapting content to stay relevant, while still ensuring that the brand's core message is maintained.

Another challenge that brands face in influencer marketing is measuring ROI. Unlike traditional advertising, where metrics like impressions and click-through rates are well-established, influencer marketing involves a broader range of outcomes, many of which are difficult to quantify. For example, the impact of an influencer campaign on brand sentiment, customer loyalty, or long-term brand awareness can be challenging to measure directly. Additionally, the influence of social media algorithms, which can affect the visibility of posts, adds another layer of complexity to tracking the effectiveness of influencer campaigns.

To address these challenges, brands must develop a comprehensive approach to measuring ROI that goes beyond basic metrics. This might involve using a combination of quantitative and qualitative measures, such as tracking engagement rates, conversions, and social media mentions, alongside customer surveys or sentiment analysis. Brands can also use tools like UTM codes, affiliate links, and unique discount codes to track the direct impact of influencer campaigns on sales. By taking a holistic approach to measurement, brands can gain a more accurate understanding of the true value of their influencer marketing efforts.

Finally, as influencer marketing continues to evolve, brands must navigate the challenge of staying ahead of emerging trends and technologies. The influencer landscape is constantly changing, with new platforms, content formats, and influencer types emerging regularly. For example, the rise of TikTok and the growing popularity of short-form video content have forced brands to rethink their influencer strategies to stay relevant. Similarly, the emergence of virtual influencers—computer-generated personas that interact with followers on social media—presents both opportunities and challenges for brands.

To stay ahead of these trends, brands must remain flexible and willing to experiment with new approaches. This might involve exploring new platforms, testing different content formats, or partnering with different types of influencers. Brands should also invest in ongoing research and development to keep up with the latest innovations in influencer marketing. By staying proactive and adaptable, brands can ensure that they remain competitive in an ever-changing landscape.

In conclusion, while influencer marketing offers significant opportunities for brands, it also presents a range of challenges that must be navigated carefully. From selecting the right influencers and ensuring content authenticity to managing legal compliance and measuring ROI, brands need to approach influencer marketing with a strategic mindset and a willingness to adapt. By understanding these challenges and developing effective strategies to address them, brands can maximize the impact of their influencer marketing efforts and build successful, long-lasting partnerships with influencers.

Conclusion

Navigating the world of influencer marketing is like walking through an ever-changing landscape. Just when you think you've mastered the terrain, a new trend, platform, or consumer behavior emerges, altering the path ahead. The journey, however, is not just about adapting to these changes; it's about anticipating them and shaping your strategy in ways that not only keep you relevant but put you at the forefront of the industry.

Throughout this exploration of influencer marketing, we've delved into various aspects that define this dynamic field. From selecting the right influencers to creating campaigns that resonate authentically with audiences, each step in the process requires a blend of creativity, strategy, and careful analysis. The essence of successful influencer marketing lies in understanding the subtle interplay between the influencer's authentic voice and the brand's message. This relationship is delicate, and when handled with care, it can produce powerful results that extend far beyond the metrics.

One of the most crucial takeaways from this journey is the importance of authenticity in influencer marketing. In a digital world saturated with content, consumers are increasingly discerning, able to spot inauthenticity from a mile away. They crave genuine connections, not just with brands, but with the influencers they follow. This has led to a shift in the influencer marketing paradigm, where the quality of engagement often trumps the quantity of followers. Brands that focus on authenticity, by partnering with influencers who share their values and who genuinely use and believe in their products, are more likely to build trust and loyalty among their target audience.

This authenticity also extends to the content itself. The most successful influencer campaigns are those where the content feels organic, as if the product or service being promoted is a natural part of the influencer's life. This is why giving influencers creative freedom is so important. Influencers know their audience better than anyone; they understand what resonates, what sparks interest, and what falls flat. By allowing them to weave your brand's message into their narrative in a way that feels true to their voice, you create a more compelling and credible campaign.

Another key element that has been emphasized is the strategic selection of influencers. The temptation to go for the influencer with the largest following is understandable but often misguided. As we've seen, micro and nano-influencers, despite their smaller followings, often deliver higher engagement rates and more targeted reach. These influencers cultivate close-knit communities where their recommendations carry significant weight. The relationship between the influencer and their audience is built on trust and mutual interests, making their endorsements particularly powerful. For brands, this means that success in influencer marketing often lies in the ability to identify and partner with the right influencers, those who can authentically connect with the desired audience on a deeper level.

Furthermore, the evolution of platforms has played a critical role in shaping influencer marketing strategies. From the visually-driven Instagram to the fast-paced world of TikTok, each platform offers unique opportunities and challenges. Understanding the strengths and nuances of each platform is essential for crafting campaigns that not only reach the intended audience but do so in a way that engages and resonates. The rise of video content, particularly short-form video, has revolutionized the way influencers connect with their followers. It's a trend that shows no signs of slowing down, with platforms continuously introducing new features to capitalize on the popularity of video. Brands that embrace this trend and experiment with new formats are more likely to capture the attention of today's consumers, who are increasingly drawn to dynamic, visually engaging content.

The role of technology in influencer marketing cannot be overstated. As artificial intelligence and machine learning continue to advance, they offer new tools for brands to enhance their influencer marketing efforts. AI-driven platforms can analyze vast amounts of data to identify influencers whose audiences align with a brand's target market, predict campaign outcomes, and even optimize content in real-time. This level of precision and efficiency is transforming the industry, enabling brands to make more informed decisions and achieve better results. However, with this technological advancement comes the challenge of maintaining the human element that is so central to influencer marketing. While AI can enhance the process, it's the human connections, the stories, and the emotions that truly resonate with audiences.

One of the more complex aspects of influencer marketing that has been explored is the legal and regulatory landscape. As the industry grows, so does the scrutiny from regulatory bodies. Compliance with guidelines around disclosure and transparency is not just a legal obligation but a crucial factor in maintaining consumer trust. The industry's ability to adapt to these regulations while continuing to deliver compelling, authentic content will be key to its sustained success. Brands must be diligent in ensuring that their influencer partnerships adhere to all legal requirements, and influencers must be educated on the importance of clear and honest communication with their followers.

The conversation around influencer marketing would be incomplete without addressing the challenges that come with measuring ROI. Unlike traditional advertising, where success can often be measured by straightforward metrics like impressions or click-through rates, the impact of influencer marketing is more nuanced. While immediate sales and conversions are important, the long-term effects on brand awareness, customer loyalty, and overall brand sentiment are equally valuable. As such, brands need to develop comprehensive measurement frameworks that capture the full spectrum of benefits that influencer marketing can offer. This might include a combination of quantitative metrics, such as engagement rates and conversion tracking, with qualitative assessments, like customer feedback and sentiment analysis.

The future of influencer marketing, as discussed, is poised to be shaped by several emerging trends. The rise of purpose-driven influencers, who use their platforms to advocate for social and environmental causes, reflects a broader shift in consumer expectations. Today's consumers are not just looking for products; they are looking for brands that align with their values. This presents both an opportunity and a challenge for brands as they navigate how to authentically integrate purpose into their influencer marketing strategies. Those that succeed will likely find that they not only attract more loyal customers but also contribute positively to the broader social conversation.

In parallel, the development of virtual influencers—computer-generated personas that interact with followers in much the same way as human influencers—introduces a fascinating new dynamic to the industry. While virtual influencers offer brands a level of control and consistency that is difficult to achieve with human influencers, they also raise questions about authenticity and connection. As this technology continues to evolve, brands will need to carefully consider how to balance the use of virtual influencers with the need for genuine, human interaction.

Ultimately, the ongoing evolution of influencer marketing reflects the broader changes in how consumers interact with brands in the digital age. It is a field that requires constant adaptation, creativity, and a deep understanding of both the influencers and the audiences they engage. The brands that will thrive are those that approach influencer marketing not just as a tactic but as a strategic, integral part of their overall marketing approach. They will recognize that the key to successful influencer marketing lies in building authentic relationships, staying ahead of trends, and continually refining their strategies to meet the ever-changing needs and expectations of their audiences.

As the landscape continues to shift, one thing remains clear: influencer marketing is here to stay. It has proven to be an incredibly effective way for brands to connect with consumers, build trust, and drive engagement. The challenge moving forward will be to maintain the delicate balance between authenticity and innovation, ensuring that as the industry grows and changes, it remains rooted in the genuine connections that have made it so successful in the first place. Brands that can navigate this balance will find themselves not just keeping pace with the industry but leading it into the future.

www.ingramcontent.com/pod-product-compliance
Lightning Source LLC
LaVergne TN
LVHW022320200926
848481LV00004B/1378
9798349537974